"WHAT CAN WE SHARE?"

BY
TRUDIAN BRAITHWAITE

Acknowledgment

I would like to express my deepest gratitude to everyone who supported me on this journey. To my children, your love and laughter inspire every word I write. To my family and friends, thank you for believing in me and encouraging my dreams.

 To the amazing families I've worked with as a nanny or night nurse ,thank you for allowing me to care for your little ones they've taught me so much about the beauty of childhood.

Finally, to all the readers who open this book, thank you for sharing this story. Your support means the world to me.

About author

Trudian, affectionately called "Tru Tru," is a devoted single mom living in the United States. A full-time nanny and night nurse with several certificates in child care services, she also holds a bachelor's degree in finance and management. Passionate about children and storytelling, Trudian brings warmth, creativity, and expertise to her work, inspiring young minds with her heartfelt tales.

Dedication

To my beautiful children, the light of my life, and to all the children who inspire us with their boundless imagination and joy. May this book bring smiles, laughter, and a reminder that love and resilience can create magic in everyday moments. This is for you, with all my heart.

Sharing is fun, and it shows we care,
But some things are special and not for us to
share.

Toys and games are fun to share,
When friends come over and play fair..

Books, puzzles, cars, and trains,
Art supplies to draw with friends again.
Sharing with friends is fun to do,
It makes everyone happy, including you!.

But there are some things just for you,
Like your toothbrush and washcloth too.
We can share the toothpaste, that's okay,
But some things are yours in a special way..

Food is something we can share,
but not when we are not feeling well.

Clothes, hats, and socks are fun to share,
But your underwear is just for you to wear
something we don't share

Feelings and stories are great to tell,
Sharing how we feel helps us feel well.

But private thoughts and secrets we keep,
Some things are for us alone, down deep.

Nose tissues are one thing we don't share,
Each of us needs our own, it's fair.

Friends and family are special, it's true,
Sharing love and kindness is the best thing to do.

We must be respectful with others' stuff,
When they share, that's fair, and it shows we care

So remember what we can share,
and what we should not,
Sharing shows we care, but some things we've got,
Are just for us, and that's okay,

Sharing makes us all feel bright,
Turns our days from dark to light.
Friends are happy, smiles we see,
Sharing spreads the joy for free. Ooooh Raaay